Cinderella

A pantomime

David Cregan

Music by
Brian Protheroe

Samuel French - London
New York - Toronto - Hollywood

CINDERELLA

First presented at the Theatre Royal, Stratford East on 4th December 1989, with the following cast:

Cinderella	Michelle Gayle
Baron Jones	Alex Richardson
Buttons	Ian Bartholomew
Samantha	Sheri Graubert
Jack	David Harewood
Queen Charlotte	Penny Nice
King James	John Halstead
Prince Hugo	Mark Haddigan
Fairy Godmother/Baroness	Geraldine Fitzgerald
Cloaca	Yvonne Edgell
Lymphida	Michelle Fine
Mrs Joy Da Palma	Michael Bertenshaw

Directed by Philip Hedley
Assistant Director Mark Thomson
Designed by Geoff Rose
Lighting by Stephen Watson
Choreographed by Karen Rabinowitz
Stage Manager Em Parkinson
Sound by Derrick Zieba
Musical Director Dave Brown
Musicians: Lyn Edwards (drums and percussion), Nick Lacey (Keyboards)

SYNOPSIS OF SCENES

MUSICAL NUMBERS

ACT I

1.	Prince's Gallope	Prince, Sam, Jack, Queen, King
2.	Skip a Bit and Smile	Buttons, Sam, Jack, Baron, Cinderella
3.	Damn Near Dead	Fairy Godmother, Buttons
4.	We Want a Skivvy	Cloaca, Lymphida, Mrs Da Palma, King, Queen, Prince, Sam, Jack
5.	I Am the Bride	Mrs Da Palma, Baron, Buttons, Sam, Jack
6.	I Can Pay My Bills	Baron, Buttons, Sam, Jack
7.	I Can't Believe	Cinderella
8.	Downtown Summer Spree	King, Queen, Prince, Sam, Jack
9.	I Have a Dream	Cinderella, chorus
10.	Simple Cinders, Delicious Girl	Fairy Godmother, chorus

ACT II

11.	The Schmaltz Waltz	Royal Family, Guests
12.	Paradise	Prince, Cinderella, Guests
13.	Proclamation	King, Prince, Guests
14.	The Dancer I'll Love	Prince
15.	Don't Wash, My Darling	Buttons, Fairy Godmother,
14.	The Dancer I'll Love (Reprise)	Buttons
16.	Come All Ye Well-shod Girls	Prince, King, Queen, Sam, Jack
17.	Shout, Shout, Shout	Buttons, Sam, Jack
18.	Be A ***	Mrs Da Palma
19.	You Can't Keep a Good Girl Down	Buttons and Company

Other Pantomimes by David Cregan, with music by Brian Protheroe:

Beauty and the Beast
Jack and the Beanstalk
Red Ridinghood
Sleeping Beauty

ACT I

SCENE 1

A bedroom at the Baron's

A bed by the fire is revealed, with the Baroness in it, the Baron beside it, Cinderella very close to her mother and Buttons hovering

Cinderella You'll soon be better, Mother. I'll make you better.
Baroness Can I have some grapes?
Cinderella Of course you can . . . Buttons?
Buttons We haven't any grapes, Cinderella, only apples. What about some apples, keep the doctor away, which is an idea, considering his price.
Baron Good heavens, yes. Try apples, my love.
Cinderella Pawn my dress to buy grapes.
Buttons I've pawned all your dresses already.
Baroness Dear Cinderella, you're the best daughter in the world, just rub my hands . . .
Cinderella They're cold. (*Alarmed*) Mother, they're cold!

Music

Baron Oh . . .
Cinderella Mother! Aaaah! (*She clasps her father*)
Baron There now. We'll manage on our own, somehow.
Cinderella We won't!
Buttons Of course we will. We'll be cheerful and bright, and laugh a lot, and do all the things the Baroness would've wanted—visits to the sea-side, mini-golf. Smile everyone.
Cinderella Why?
Buttons Life has to go on!
Cinderella Why?
Buttons Because it has. (*To the audience*) I have a very difficult part in this story. There are times when I wish I was somewhere else. In service at the Palace, for example. Things are more lively there, I'll bet!

SCENE 2

The throne room at the palace

Lots of light, gigantic and jolly trumpets

Sam, a tomboy girl and Jack enter, both on horseback

As the trumpets finish, the old and wild-looking Queen Charlotte enters

Sam
Jack } (*together*) Silence for Her Majesty The Queen!

Queen And where's His Majesty the King?

King (*off*) Here, my love.

More immense trumpets

   The old and wild-looking King James enters and interrupts the trumpets

   Thank you, that'll do.

Queen (*to Sam and Jack*) And you'll get scratch marks on the marble.

King Where's Prince Hugo?

Queen Our son.

Sam He's saddling up.

King Before breakfast?

Jack He rides to breakfast nowadays.

King He rides everywhere.

Queen Something must be done, James.

King He must get married.

Sam
Jack } (*together*) Oh no.

Queen Oh yes.

King Hugo!

Queen Hugo!

Prince (*off*) Coming.

King I wish he were forty-five and sensible.

   Prince Hugo enters on horseback with the Company

Song 1: Prince's Gallope

All the Young   We're ever so happy and sporty
And given to slapping our thighs.
We're handsome and dashing and naughty,
With wicked and wonderful eyes.
If sometimes we're rather alarming
At least we are never a bore.
We're led by a prince who is charming
And we're awfully nice to the poor.

Chorus
Tally ho! tally ho!
It's a hunting that we go!

Though we mess up the countryside
                     rotten
We at least make a wonderful show.
Toot de too
View halloo
We are noble strong and true.
Tantivvy, tantivvy, tantivvy—
And we're nice, so sucks to you.

Prince   As a prince I am busy as busy
With some of my very best chums
Doing things that are daring and dizzy
To banish the glooms and the glums.
If we frighten the cows when they're
                              grazing
And keep all the sheep on the run,
We're just being young and amazing,
And it's all jolly good fun.

Chorus
Tally ho! Tally ho!
It's a hunting that we go!
Though we rather get up people's noses
We are awfully amusing to know.
Toot de too
View halloo
We're on every Christmas view
Tantivvy, tantivvy, tantivvy—
And we're nice, frightfully nice, nice
                            as nice
So sucks to you.

Braying laughter

Queen You say it this time, James.
King Something Must Be Done.
Queen Now.
Prince Hallo, Ma.
Queen (*escaping horse and rider*) Take that thing away.

Braying laughter from friends

Prince So sorry. Hallo, Pa.
King (*also escaping*) Stop it! Stop it!
Prince I expect he thinks you're a sugar lump.

Braying laughter from friends

King You must get married and be serious.
Prince and Friends What?
Prince I'm having too much fun, and I'm doing a tremendous lot of good,
spreading joy and that.
King Where, for heaven's sake?
Prince Among the Less Fortunate, and they think I'm absolutely splendid.
Sam You are absolutely splendid.
Jack We're all absolutely splendid.
Sam And people love us.
Jack Isn't it nice?
King You must get to know some girls.
Sam I'm a girl, actually, aren't I, Jack?
Jack Yes, you are Sam.

King It's news to me.

Queen And we can't have a future queen called Sam because people will be surprised.

Prince Well I'm going to be a bachelor for ever and ever, and have fun doing good things among the Less Fortunate, and that's that.

Prince, Sam, Jack Yes! (*They slap their thighs*)

King But we want to retire.

Queen We want to stop being King and Queen.

Prince Don't be silly old parents. Just have a nice day ruling the kingdom while I go and Be Helpful.

King Foiled again, Charlotte.

All　　　　　　　Tally ho! Tally ho!
　　　　　　　　　We're full of fun you know.

　　　　　　　　　We're none of us into marriage,
　　　　　　　　　It's a terrible way to go.
　　　　　　　　　Toot de too
　　　　　　　　　View halloo,
　　　　　　　　　We're away to pastures new.
　　　　　　　　　Tantivvy, tantivvy, tantivvy,
　　　　　　　　　And we're nice, nice as nice,
　　　　　　　　　　　　　　　　frightfully nice
　　　　　　　　　So sucks to you!

SCENE 3

A wood or some outdoor place

Prince Hugo, Sam and Jack are prancing on their horses at the end of the last chorus

The Baron, Buttons, and Cinderella enter pulling a coffin on a cart

Prince Now, what have we here, then?

Jack Oh dear.

Sam Oh dear.

Jack Oh Lord.

Prince It's the Less Fortunate. Three of them.

Sam Four of them, actually. And one of them is much Less Fortunate than the others.

Jack About as Un-fortunate as you can get, I'd say, ah ha ha.

Prince Hallo, there. This—er—this is a pretty unhappy picture you make.

Baron Yes, it is.

Buttons It's the Baron's wife, sir. That's the Baron, Baron Jones, and his daughter, Cinderella Jones, and his wife, the Baroness, she's in here.

Prince Oh dear.

Buttons Dead.

Prince Oh, well, that's something.
Buttons The pneumonia did it, and the doctor's bills were shocking.
Prince Really?
Buttons Took all our money, all Cinderella's dresses, the family portraits, the horses—you are the nice kind prince aren't you, famous for his generosity?
Prince Er——
Buttons Well, the horses went, all the lovely prancing horses.
Sam
Jack } (*together*) Not the horses.
Prince You poor people. They say the Baroness was such a jolly lady.
Sam Awfully good parties, I'm told.
Jack Ice-cream, jellies, whoopee cushions . . .
Sam Aha, aha, aha.
Prince Baron Jones, would you—er—perhaps this would help with your—er . . . (*He hands over a bag of money*)
Baron Oh, thank you, sir, it would sir, thank you very much indeed, sir.
Buttons What a wonderful surprise, you nice kind prince, you.
Prince Not at all. And do remember, every cloud has a silver lining.
Jack Yes, a silver lining.
Prince And things often turn out really very nicely indeed. Goodbye. Oh, it's wonderful being helpful!
Buttons Byee. One born every minute.

The Prince canters off

Sam and Jack are about to follow but are halted by the following

Cinderella You may think it's wonderful, but I don't!
Jack What?
Sam What?
Baron We do need the cash, my dear, and I can tell you this is very wonderful in that direction.
Cinderella Cash won't bring Mother back, will it? She's gone for ever.
Baron Yes, well, that is true.
Sam Yes, it is.
Jack Is it?
Sam I should think so.
Jack I hadn't thought of that.
Cinderella I want to be really, really miserable for a bit. I don't want to think about silver linings.
Baron I do understand, but don't you see——
Cinderella I don't think you understand at all.
Baron Life has to go on. Buttons, you explain it.
Buttons (*to the audience*) I told you, I have a very difficult part in this story.
Jack Yes, you do.
Sam Impossible, I should say.
Buttons But I don't give up. Come on Cinders, it's your lovely old Buttons here, and . . .

Song 2: Skip a Bit and Smile

(*Singing*)	I understand exactly You're gloomy, glum and low. You're overwhelmed with tearfulness, Unhappiness and woe. But if you look around you For the help that fortune sends You'll find that there is comfort from Your kind well-meaning friends. If the sky is falling in
Sam, Jack, Baron }	Sky is falling in
Buttons	And you're miserable as sin
Sam, Jack Baron }	Miserable as sin
Buttons	'Cos you've lost your kith and kin
Sam, Jack Baron }	Lost your kith and kin
Buttons	Skip a bit and smile!
Sam, Jack Baron }	Lalalalalala
Buttons	If you simply can't be brave
Sam, Jack Baron }	Simply can't be brave
Buttons	Find it hard to laugh and wave
Sam, Jack Baron }	Hard to laugh and wave
Buttons	'Cos your mother's in her grave
Sam, Jack Baron }	Mother's in her grave
Buttons	Skip a bit and smile!
Middle eight	
All (*bar Cinderella*)	Don't be a whinger or a weeper Your eyes aren't pretty when they're red. We all have to meet the Great Reaper, And then when we do we'll be a long time dead.
Buttons	So if life is short of hope
Sam, Jack Baron }	Life is short of hope
Buttons	And you're on the slipp'ry slope
Sam, Jack Baron }	On the slipp'ry slope
Buttons	Busy looking for a rope
Sam, Jack Baron }	Looking for a rope

Buttons	Skip a bit and smile!
Sam, Jack ∖ **Baron** ∣	Lalalalalala.

Dance break

Cinderella	If you're lonely and alone
Others	Lonely and alone
Cinderella	'Cos the dearest friend you've known
Others	Dearest friend you've known
Cinderella	Has just left you on your own
Others	Left you on your own
Cinderella	Weep away and cry.
	If you're deeply, deeply sad
Others	Deeply, deeply sad
Cinderella	And your dearly loving dad
Others	Dearly loving dad
Cinderella	Cheers you up and drives you mad
Others	Up and drives you mad
Cinderella	Weep away and cry.

The others sing the middle eight

Others	It's only that we want to make it better.
	It's gloom that we're anxious to attack.
Cinderella	But my eyes just grow a little wetter
	With the tears for my mother who
	just won't come back.
	And I want you all to know
Others	She wants us all to know
Cinderella	That I loved my mother so
Others	She loved her mother so
Cinderella	And I simply want to go
Others	Simply want to go
Cinderella	To weep away, weep away and cry.

She goes off pushing the coffin

Baron Well, I feel the same, but life actually does have to go on, and it does have to be paid for.

He follows her off

Buttons Not exactly a wow that, still, thank you for your help, gentlemen.
Sam I'm a lady, actually.
Buttons Really?
Sam Yes, really, Bellhop.

Sam and Jack go off

Buttons (*calling*) I'm the Personal Assistant to the Baron! Buttons P.A.! Some people. (*He starts to leave*)

SCENE 4

Frontcloth

Buttons is leaving

A flash. The Fairy Godmother enters, spectacles on a string round her neck, carrying a file

Fairy Godmother Young man. Young man!

Buttons Me?

Fairy Godmother Yes, you.

Buttons Thank you—that cloak—who are you?

Fairy Godmother I'm an official Fairy Godmother, and I'm looking for the home of Cinderella Jones.

Buttons Oh, for a moment—goodness—well, you're just the thing we need ...

Fairy Godmother We?

Buttons I'm the Joneses' little treasure, their nice little man—Buttons, bright and breezy, ever so easy, more like a zip fastener, but actually Buttons.

Fairy Godmother You aren't mentioned here. (*In the file she carries*)

Buttons Well, I'm hardly worth mentioning really, because they're so deep in gloom they're beyond me.

Fairy Godmother "Deep in gloom" isn't bad enough to get help from *me*, I'm afraid.

Buttons But we need you, (*to the audience*) don't we? Louder. There, you see?

Fairy Godmother I'm simply here to keep an eye on the girl, Cinderella, until things get worse.

Buttons How much worse?

Fairy Godmother Infinitely much worse. And when they do, send for me and I will then pull out a real corker and change things amazingly. In the meantime you'll have to forget everything I've said. (*She waves her wand*)

Buttons Hallo, who are you?

Fairy Godmother I'm the Fairy Godmother. (*She waves her wand*)

Buttons Hallo, who are you?

Fairy Godmother I'm the Fairy Godmother. (*She waves her wand*)

Buttons Hallo, who are you?

Fairy Godmother (*laughing happily*) So silly, but one of the perks of the job. I'm the Fairy Godmother, and remember that, deep down inside, so that when things get absolutely frightful for Cinderella you can call me up.

Buttons Why can't I call you up now?

Fairy Godmother Because it has been decided at the highest level that nowadays magic must be cut down to one good trick for each miserable person, and that is all. The Chief Godmother has said it—suffering is good for the soul!

Song 3: Damn Near Dead

(*Singing*) We used to cure warts on the nose in
                                                 a trice,
And pimples were simple, and piles.
We'd mend broken hearts and do tricks
                                 with white mice,
And shower sweet people with smiles.
But games of that nature became such
                                                 a craze
That orders were sent from aloft;
"Be more economical, girls, in your ways,
Or the world will go weedy and soft."

Chorus
It has to be frightfully bad, my dears,
Before you can call on me.
You can't just be soulful and sad, my dears,
It has to be true misery.
You'll have to be pretty far gone, my dears,
When all has been done and said.
To yell for a spell is quite simply not on,
Unless you are damn near dead.

You might think a dragon would merit a call,
And you'd scream and you'd howl and
                                    you'd cry,
But I'm sorry, it simply won't do, not at all,
Until you are starting to fry.

Buttons When caught by a giant whose hunger is great
And likes to eat children for lunch,
Although she's observed your distress she
                                    will wait
Until he has started to crunch.

Both *Chorus, as above, prefixed by the word "Oh." Then:–*
It has to be frightfully bad, my dears,
Before you can call on me,
You can't just be soulful and sad, my dears,
It has to be true misery.
It has to go really that far, my dears,
The world's not a feather bed.
To earn a good turn from your dear godmama,
You have to be damn near dead.

Reprise chorus

Fairy Godmother So, remember, deep down, call on me when things get absolutely frightful. And in the meantime forget everything I've said. (*She waves her wand*)
Buttons Hallo, who are you?
Fairy Godmother (*looking round carefully*) I'm a person with sweeties. Here,

have some to help you remember later on. (*She gives sweets to Buttons and the children*) Goodbye till I'm needed.

The Fairy Godmother exits

Buttons How very curious.

Buttons exits

SCENE 5

The throne room

Mrs Joy Da Palma enters, tight bun and stylish, heavy lipstick, together with her daughters, Cloaca and Lymphida, who carry a cupboard between them

Mrs Da Palma Door open, nobody about—bring that cupboard here girls, and don't complain.
Lymphida Get a move on, Cloaca.
Cloaca I'll go as slow as I want.
Lymphida My arms are dropping off.
Cloaca Good.
Lymphida Mam, she said good about my arms dropping off.
Cloaca Liar.
Lymphida Mam, she said liar.
Cloaca Well, you are.
Lymphida Mam, I'm not.
Cloaca Mam, she is.
Lymphida I'm not, Mam.
Mrs Da Palma Don't show yourselves up, there are people here.
Cloaca Weedykins.
Lymphida Bullyknobs.
Cloaca Crybaby.
Lymphida Mam——
Mrs Da Palma (*to the audience*) Good-evening. I am a very rich woman but careful with it, which is why I travel by public transport. I've been far and wide looking for a suitable husband for myself, two for my daughters, and I'm sick to death of it, so now I'm prepared to settle almost for anyone. This is called Cloaca——
Cloaca 'Llo.
Mrs Da Palma —and this is called Lymphida——

Lymphida giggles

Cloaca Tch.
Lymphida Shut up.
Mrs Da Palma —and they're very, very, lovely. My name is Mrs Joy Da Palma, and I am like I said, shrewd. Where are we now, I wonder?

Prince Hugo enters on his horse, followed by Sam and Jack—they are not on horses

Lymphida Mam, a horse!
Cloaca And a throne!
Mrs Da Palma And a dish! Good-evening, young fellow, and what do you do for a living?
Prince I'm a prince.
Cloaca Ooh, Mam, can I have him?
Lymphida I want him.
Cloaca You had the seat nearest the window in the coach.
Lymphida You had the wetting doll at Christmas.
Cloaca You had the last piece of nougat yesterday.
Lymphida Mam, she's at it again.
Cloaca I'm not. It's my turn and I want the Prince.
Lymphida I want the Prince.
Mrs Da Palma I want the Prince, and you disasters keep quiet or you'll go in the cupboard!

A little silence

Cloaca (*to Lymphida*) See what you've done.
Lymphida Be nice to us, Mam.
Mrs Da Palma I'll be nice if you will.
Prince Are you three some of the Less Fortunate?
Mrs Da Palma Indeed we are, sir. I am a lonely widow looking for somewhere suitable to perch.
Prince (*having an idea*) Ah! A *rich* widow?
Sisters Yes.
Mrs Da Palma Do you need a rich one? Mm?
Prince Someone does, eh Sam? Jack?
Lymphida What are they?
Sam I'm a girl.
Jack And I prefer horses.
Prince What about sending this lady off to marry poor Baron Jones, eh? He needs a wife.
Sam Not that wife.
Jack It's a rotten idea.
Prince But she's got money.
Lymphida (*holding up a bag*) In here.
Mrs Da Palma Quiet.
Prince And money's what the Baron's awfully short of.
Sam The Joneses are very sensitive.
Jack Especially Cinderella.
Prince Is that the grubby daughter?
Sam She's not grubby; she's upset.

  The King and Queen enter

King (*delighted*) Girls! Look Charlotte, girls!
Queen Just what's needed.
Mrs Da Palma And who are you?
Cloaca Apart from being moth-eaten.

King We're the King.
Queen And the Queen.
Mrs Da Palma Oh, I'm so sorry. (*She grovels*)

Trumpets begin

King (*to the trumpets*) Stop it. Did they let you in?
Mrs Da Palma The door was open.
King Well, since you're here let me tell you we want to retire and start life afresh so perhaps one of you would marry Prince Hugo and settle him down.
Mrs Da Palma
Lymphida } (*together*) Oh, I will!
Cloaca
Prince No, no, no. Send them to the Joneses. Careful, Dobbin. Steady, boy.
Lymphida He's nibbling my bustle!
Cloaca First the bustle, then the gristle, ha ha ha!!

The horse turns on her

Oh! Get him off, Mam!
Mrs Da Palma Quiet!
Prince He thinks you're a bit of apple, I expect.
Queen They're very noisy for girls, James.
Mrs Da Palma Sire! Hold your horse!
King That's the Prince, madam. Be polite to him and say please.
Mrs Da Palma Your Majesty, forgive me.
King If your manners ......
Mrs Da Palma Please tell me about these Joneses. A baron, you say.
Prince With a very jolly house, and a sort of butler thing, and a poor little daughter.
Sam (*to Jack*) Stop him.
Jack Hugo, no.
Mrs Da Palma Well, an older man is easier to manage than a young one, so, lead me to him without more ado.
Cloaca It sounds just what we want, Mam.
Lymphida Especially with a poor little daughter to wait on us.
Cloaca Yes, a poor little daughter to wait on us.
Lymphida We can shout at her, like a slave.
Cloaca And boss her about, like a skivvy.
Lymphida And put her in the cupboard if she's naughty, and pull the dreaded silence lever.
Cloaca We can play at being Mother. (*Horrid laugh*)
King Don't you want anything else out of life?
Cloaca Yes. Everything.

Song 4: We Want a Skivvy

Sisters   We want beds of gooses' feathers,
                       We want sheets of gold lamé.
                       We want satins silks and leathers,

Anti-pong stuff from Cathay,
We want quail's eggs with our coffee,
Clotted cream poured in our tea.
We want tons of treacle toffee,
And on top of all that we ...

Chorus
Want a skivvy, skivvy, skivvy, skivvy.
To scrub the bath, wash up and clean
                  the privy.
We want someone in a skirt
We can boss around and hurt,
And who'll never answer back because
She knows she's only dirt.
That's a skivvy, that's a skivvy,

Others   Oh, poor skivvy!

Sisters   So give us, give us, give us please a skivvy.
One thing more than any other
That we want my darling Mother,
Is a lousey, blousey, frousey little
                  skivvy.

Mrs Da Palma   You shall have one dears, with pleasure,
Just to do with as you choose.
You can scold her at your leisure,
And upbraid her to amuse.
You can show her that you're spiteful
With a touch of cruelty.
It will make your days delightful
And keep *you* away from *me* ...
Chorus

Sisters   Oh a skivvy, skivvy, skivvy, skivvy,
Mrs Da Palma   To scrub the bath, wash up and clean
                  the privy.
We want someone in a skirt
We can boss around and hurt
A miserable child to chase and
                  chivvy,

Mrs Da Palma   If she's idle or she's slack
You can give her shins a whack.
She'll be wonderfully loyal,

Sisters   And if not she'll get the sack.
Others   Not a skivvy, you can't beat a humble
                  skivvy.
Mrs Da Palma   Nothing whimpers quite so meekly as a
                  skivvy.
You can practise being grown up,
Be unfair and never own up,
With a faithful, cowardy custard little
                  skivvy.

Last chorus

Sisters   Skivvy, skivvy, skivvy, skivvy,
Mrs Da Palma   A downright dreadful dreary little divi.
                     She'll spoil us all day long,
                     And if ever she goes wrong,
                     Or makes a mess of something we
                     Will beat her like a gong.
Others   We must protest you shall
                     Not have a skivvy.
Sisters   }
Mrs Da Palma } A slobby, yobby, snotty, spotty skivvy.
Sisters   We'll pass our days in laughter,
                     And be happy ever after,
                     With a skivvy, skivvy, skivvy, skivvy, skivvy.

Queen They're horrible.

King Take them away, Hugo.

Prince They're not exactly lovable but they'll do very well for the Joneses.

Sam You can't do that.

Prince Oh, it'll be all right. The Less Fortunate always get on well together, it's their thing. Lead them to the Joneses straight away and no more arguing.

King From anyone.

Mrs Da Palma Take up your cupboard, girls, and walk. Thank you, sire.

Lymphida It's the skivvy cupboard now, Mam.

Cloaca It's the skivvy cupboard.

Lymphida That's the silence lever.

Cloaca The silence lever.

Queen Just go, will you. Sam and Jack, or whatever you are, take them away.

Sam and Jack escort the three off

Prince That's that tidied up.

King Leave us with the same old problem, Charlotte. Oooh, ow, get that animal away from me.

Prince Hugo and the King leave

Queen (*to the audience*) Hugo seems to have no instinct for making a home.

She leaves

Scene 6

Outside the Baron's house

Buttons and Cinderella are finishing the painting of the outside of the house

Buttons There. It looks lovely, doesn't it.

Cinderella (*still gloomy*) I suppose so.
Buttons Yes, it does. Come on, it does. (*He starts a mock sword-fight with Cinderella using the paint brushes*)
Cinderella Stop it. Stop it! Oh, you silly Buttons.

He dabs her on the cheek

Buttons A hit, a hit, a palpable hit. Buttons, the great swordsman, always gets his man or woman.

While he is showing off, Cinderella gets him one with her own brush

Ah, a cowardly, dastardly low and beastly blow on the bot, by George!

They chase each other and finally hug

Cinderella Oh, silly old Buttons.
Buttons Oh, silly old Cinders.

The Baron enters with papers and worry

Baron Bills, bills, bills, I don't know. And you've squandered all the Prince's money on the house.
Buttons Not squandered, Baron. The house is a vision of loveliness and cheer.

Mrs Da Palma enters with her daughters and Sam and Jack

Mrs Da Palma A home of character and charm, recently renovated, garden laid to lawn, I think I'll have it.
Baron What?
Cinderella What?
Buttons What?
Sisters Oh goody.
Mrs Da Palma And this, I take it, is the skivvy.
Cinderella The skivvy?
Sam (*angry*) It's Cinderella!
Jack Who is very sensitive.
Cloaca And a mess. Take our bags.
Lymphida And wash your face.
Cloaca And stand up straight.
Lymphida And always say "Yes, ma'am".
Cloaca And get us some orangeade with ice and lemon and a bit of mint, now, go on, get it!
Lymphida } (*together*) Skivvy
Cloaca
Cinderella I won't!
Baron That's my daughter.
Cloaca She's dirty.
Lymphida And she's filthy.
Cloaca And a real-bad mannered slob. (*She kicks Cinderella*)
Buttons You clear out, you dustbinful of nastiness.
Cloaca Mam!

Buttons I don't know who you are, but this is Baron Jones's daughter and
my friend and you are scumbags and snotties.
Mrs Da Palma They're my daughters!
Buttons Then trade them in for something better before anyone notices.
Jack Oh, well done.
Sam Dear Buttons.
Buttons It's nothing.
Mrs Da Palma Baron Jones?
Baron Yes.
Mrs Da Palma I've been sent here on the orders of the Prince to marry you.
Cinderella No.
Buttons No.
Mrs Da Palma Show him the money, Lymphida.

Lymphida does. He is amazed

Baron Oh heavens.
Mrs Da Palma And those are your bills?
Baron Yes.
Mrs Da Palma Forget them. Run along and choose some nice rooms for us,
dears. I'm going to pay the bills so I'm going to take charge. Skivvy, show
them round.
Cinderella I will not.
Mrs Da Palma Oh, yes you will.
Buttons (*with the audience, Jack and Sam*) Oh no she won't.

Et cetera

Mrs Da Palma I see we have troublemakers among us. Go and choose your
rooms on your own, then, darlings.
Sisters Yippee We will.

They rush off

Cinderella No!

She runs off after them

Mrs Da Palma Oh look, she's doing what I told her after all.
Jack Baron, this is not the sort of lady you should marry.
Sam No, it isn't.
Buttons You can say that again—and again.
Jack If you really need a wife you could marry *her*. (*He indicates Sam*)
Sam Yes, I'm a girl.
Mrs Da Palma Can you pay his bills?
Sam No.
Baron You see? She *is* the sort of lady I should marry.
Mrs Da Palma So, propose, and get the liquidity you long for.
Baron Madam, will you do me the honour to be my wife?
Jack Baron!
Mrs Da Palma Certainly.
Sam Think of Cinderella.

Buttons You don't even know her name!
Mrs Da Palma My name is Joy. What's yours?
Baron George.
Mrs Da Palma Well, hallo George, and welcome aboard, as they say.

Song 5: I Am the Bride

(*Singing*)   I am the bride.
                      I'll take you in my stride.
                      If you disapprove of how I run things
                      Woe betide
                      I'll hold the purse,
                      For better or for worse.
                      Will you have me?
Baron   Yes, I'll have you.

As the two kiss distantly ...

Buttons)
Sam   } Curse, curse, curse.
Jack   )

Music continues under

Mrs Da Palma (*speaking*) When I move, I move fast.

  She goes, laughing

  We'll see a lawyer later.
Buttons What on earth do you think you're doing?

Song 6: I Can Pay My Bills

Baron   I can pay my bills,
                      I'm a solvent little chappie.
                      There's a sound of tills,
                      Ringing up in all the stores.
                      I can buy all things
                      To make Cinderella happy,
                      And my old heart sings
                      As my grief withdraws.

                      Chorus
                      Heigh ho,
                      We're free.
                      We can live without a worry
                      As a happy family.
                      What joy
                      Is there
                      To spend a bit on luxury
                      And just not care.
Buttons   You're a daft old bat

Sam, Jack	There'll be awful consequences.
	She's a sly old rat
	With a cobra's jolly grin.
	She's a tongue like fire
	That will lacerate your senses,
	And you might expire
	To escape the din.
Baron	Oh no.
Others	Oh yes.
Baron	We will live without a worry
Others	For an hour or less,
Baron	Not so,
	You'll see.
	Our honeymoon will linger to eternity.
	'Cos I can pay my bills
Others	There'll be awful consequences
Baron	There's a sound of tills
Others	With a cobra's jolly grin.
	She's a tongue of fire
Baron	To make Cinderella happy
Others	And you might expire
Baron	But I can pay my——

Mrs Da Palma enters

Mrs Da Palma George, don't sing. (*She smiles*) And will you leave us to discuss our family affairs?
Jack Yes.
Sam If we must.

They go

Mrs Da Palma (*no smile*) Now, please come and stop your daughter claiming the best bedroom.
Baron But it's hers.
Mrs Da Palma It's mine.

The Baron opens his mouth

I'm in charge.

Cinderella bursts in

Cinderella She says you've married her.
Baron For your sake as much as anything.
Cinderella She stinks, and so do her brats.
Mrs Da Palma You—get in that cupboard until you're nice.
Cinderella No.
Buttons No.

The sisters appear either at windows or at the door

Cloaca Force her to go in, Mam.

Lymphida In the dark.
Cloaca Pull the silence lever.
Cinderella I am nice, and I won't go.
Buttons Don't go. (*He works up the audience*)
Mrs Da Palma Troublemakers, I knew it. There'll be more about this later. (*To the sisters*) Make yourselves completely at home, girls. From now on, Cinderella will be sleeping in the kitchen. And Lymphida, have a bath.

She leaves

Cloaca I'm going to put stones in your shoes, skivvy.
Lymphida And make you run up and downstairs.

They retire giggling

Buttons How could you do it? You don't deserve to be a father.
Cinderella You've given everything away. How could you?

Song 7: I Can't Believe

(*Singing*)   I can't believe I'll sleep tonight
                    Hard on the kitchen floor.
                    I can't believe you'll let me stay there
                    Now and ever more.
                    I can't believe you've let me go,
                    No more to laugh and play.
                    I can't believe that you can simply
                    Give my home away.
Baron (*speaking*) I did it for you, Cinderella, I did.

As the second verse is sung Cinderella's bedclothes are thrown out of the window

Cinderella   I can't believe your gift is just
                    To scold at every turn,
                    I can't believe you've sold me into
                    Slav'ry sharp and stern.
                    I can't believe you've made my life
                    So cold and dark and grey
                    I can't believe that you can simply
                    Give my home away.
Mrs Da Palma (*speaking, off*) George, come and kiss your new daughters good-night.

The Baron goes as ...

Lymphida (*off*) Does he have to, slobbery old thing?
Buttons I'll buy you something to make up for it, Cinders. I'll buy you a pumpkin. I wonder why I said that.
Cinderella I'm so unhappy.

Reprise of "I Can't Believe"

(*Singing*)   I can't believe I'll never feel
My pillow warm at night,
Or wake to see my bedroom window
Glow in the morning light.
I can't believe that now my life's
So cold and dark and grey.
I can't believe that he can simply
Give my home away
My home away.

SCENE 7

Frontcloth

The Fairy Godmother enters

Fairy Godmother I'm not going to do anything yet, but two months have passed, and things are going exactly as expected. Very badly. (*She chuckles*) In a few minutes you'll see how really very unkindly poor Cinderella is being treated, but first, I'm trying to get a bit of influence at the palace. I've got a tiny bit of magic saved up from another job I did—a rather nasty business with a beast who wouldn't turn nice when kissed— and I might have enough to put a thought into the mind of a certain person who is not as cheerful as he was. The Prince. His friends won't talk to him. He's given up horses and he's deeply dejected. Watch.

She waves the frontcloth away and leaves

SCENE 8

The throne room

The Prince is banging his head on the throne. The King and Queen are distracted. Sam and Jack are standing pointedly with their backs to the Prince

King Take up golf, then.
Queen Try bird-watching.
King Gardening.
Queen Bees.
King Trees.
Queen Beetles.
Both Anything.
Prince No-one will talk to me. Sam? Jack? You can play with my Yo-Yo.
Sam Don't want to.
Jack You've made life awful for the Joneses and we hate you.
Prince I was trying to help.
Jack Well, you failed.

Sam Failed.
Prince All *right*.
Jack They're utterly dismal.
Prince All *right!*
King You could get married.
Prince No!

A magic sound. The echoing voice of the Fairy Godmother

Fairy Godmother (*off*) What about a ball?
King Who said that?
Prince A ball?
Sam We haven't had a ball in years.
Queen The chandeliers are cracked and the harp's broken.
Fairy Godmother (*off, as before*) A ball, have a ball!
King It's an idea. There'd be girls, real ones with proper names.
Queen (*realizing the implications*) Oh yes!
Jack She has a proper name.
Prince It's a splendid idea, let's do it!
All Here. Next Tuesday!

Song 8: Downtown Summer Spree

King
Queen } (*together*) Well, come along down to the palace, honey
Going to have a ball, chase the blues
                                    away.
Going to pawn the crown if we're
                                    short of money,
We're going to dance,
Till the skies turn sunny,
We're going to glitter like sequins,
                                    baby,
Wear a fancy garter with the OBE
We'll have to throw that orb away,
And let the saucy sceptre sway,
At the old Prince Charming downtown
                                    summer spree.

Change of rhythm

All   Where we'll have rhumbas
To shake our bumbas,
And we'll have tangos for those with expertise,
And we'll do congas
For just as long as
Our hips will go on wagging
Without sagging to our knees.
So—
Come along down to the throne room, people,
Come and cut a rug make the ermine hop,

Listen how the boop-de-boop and beep'll
Ring.
W' a swing
From the old church steeple!

Dance break

Things old and sweet as
The dear veletas
And waltzes so stately and sure,
So romantic, and unfrantic,
You can dance them with ease as you snore.

So come along down to the palace, honey
Come and have a ball, chase the blues away,
Going to pawn the crown if we're short of money
We're gonna dance
Till the skies turn sunny
So jitter-bug and jive round the dais, baby,
Do the bug-a-boogie with the King and Queen
And let the cobwebs blow away
And let the saucy sceptre sway,
At the old Prince Charming downtown summer
                                                   spree—yeah!

King Right, let's get going. Balloons, a band, invitations.
Sam Invitations.
Queen Food.
Jack Food.
Prince Polish my medals.
Sam You can do that.
Queen And Hugo, you must promise me one thing.
Prince Yes Ma?
Queen At this ball try, just try, to fall in love.
Prince Oh Ma, you always spoil things. (*He starts to leave*)
King You might quite like it.

   The Prince, King and Queen leave

Sam I would.
Jack Who'd you fall in love with?
Sam I'm not sure.
Jack You do have strange ideas at times.

SCENE 9

The kitchen at the Jones's

Cinderella's bed is in one corner

Cinderella is on the floor, scrubbing

Mrs Da Palma is standing over her

Mrs Da Palma Come on, do it thoroughly, really work on those bristles.
Cinderella I am doing.
Mrs Da Palma Don't lie to me. Scrub till it hurts, then clean the pots.
Cinderella I have done.
Mrs Da Palma And polish the windows.
Cinderella I will.
Mrs Da Palma You should've done them already but I suppose you've been
idling away in bed, like your father.

Cloaca enters

Cloaca Lymph is being sick again.
Mrs Da Palma Then go and mop it up, Skivvy.
Cinderella The windows——
Cloaca The dining-room floor's all horrid and yellow. Tell her, Mam.

Buttons enters

Buttons She's done it again. Puke-ho, my hearties. Too much chocky before
breakfast.

He takes the mop which is passed round to the requisite person in the following

Mrs Da Palma She'll go.
Cinderella (*taking the mop back*) You clean the windows.
Cloaca She'll clean the windows later.
Buttons (*taking the mop*) Then I'll mop the dining-room.
Mrs Da Palma You'll do nothing.
Buttons (*passing the mop*) Then you'll mop the dining-room, I'll do
nothing, she'll clean the windows.
Mrs Da Palma (*passing the mop*) She'll mop the dining-room, you'll do
nothing, and I'll clean the windows.
Cloaca That's not right, Mam.
Mrs Da Palma What's not right?
Buttons She's quite right, you're not right, she'll (*Cloaca*) mop the dining-
room, (*passing the mop*) I'll clean the windows and you'll do nothing as
usual.
Mrs Da Palma You'll go in the cupboard.
Buttons (*moving the mop again*) Cloaca'll go in the cupboard, you'll mop the
dining-room., I'll clean the windows and Cinders'll do nothing.
Mrs Da Palma } (*together*) She always does nothing.
Cloaca
Mrs Da Palma Mop the dining-room.

Lymphida enters

Lymphida Mam, I've been sick.
Cloaca Get away from me.
Cinderella Sit here, Lymphida, and rest in case you're sick again.
Lymphida Why should I?

Cinderella Because you don't like being sick.
Lymphida She's being nice to me, Mam. What do I do?
Cloaca Kick her.

Mrs Da Palma and the sisters hoot with laughter. Buttons seizes the mop. He makes buzzing sounds

Buttons Oh! A hornet, a horrid hornet. It's on your neck, Lymphida. There! (*He wallops Lymphida on the neck with the mop*)
Lymphida Aaah! (*She gags*)
Buttons Missed it. Oh, cork that sick up. (*He puts a dishcloth in her mouth*)
Cloaca I don't believe there's a hornet.
Buttons OK—(*he buzzes*)—there is, there is! (*He makes dive-bombing noises. A blow of the mop on Cloaca*) Missed. (*Blow of mop*) Missed again. (*Blow of mop*) And still it avoids the fearless Buttons.
Cloaca (*escaping*) Help! Heeeeelp!

She's off

Mrs Da Palma I know what you're doing, Buttonss. You don't fool me.
Buttons It's after you now, circling your head, deciding whether to attack the nose or chin. Aaah. (*He lunges*)
Mrs Da Palma (*as she runs off screaming*) I'll have you in the cupboard for this.

Mrs Da Palma exits

Buttons (*to Lymphida*) Taste nice?

Lymphida shakes her head

You know where that hornet is now, I suppose. You'd better take your clothes off before it gives you a big boil on the er …
Lymphida I can't take them off here.
Buttons That's up to you.
Lymphida Mam, there a hornet in my unmentionables and I'm going to be sick.

Lymphida goes

Cinderella (*with a pile of washing*) Oh, Buttons. You're the only thing that makes life worth living. Why d'you stay?
Buttons Because I love you.
Cinderella I love you, too.
Buttons You mean, you mean properly?
Cinderella Yes, of course. But I wonder what it's like to be loved by someone really important?
Buttons Oh—well, I expect it's very nice.
Cinderella I have a dream that one day all this will end. One day I really will be loved, by everyone, really hugely.
Buttons You're loved fairly hugely already, actually.
Cinderella One day, Buttons, I will matter.

Song 9: I Have a dream

(*Singing*)   I have a dream that is rich with friends,
Friends who have sought me and found me.
Life there is playtime that never ends
Laughter echoing round me.
Picnics happen in the boundless hay,
Fresh jam sandwiches for tea.
When the sun begins to fade away
Stories are told at somebody's knee.
I have a dream that I am happy there,
Comfy with people who are kind.
In the midst of my dream, though, I am
                                    lonely,
For the dream is just in my mind.

Chorus (*off*)   Ah Ah Ah Ah Ah.

Cinderella   I have a dream which is full of folk,
Loving and smiling and gentle.
People who came around to share a joke
Nice, and awfully sentimental.
Summer settles in an endless haze,
Like it used to long ago.
Folks have manners and the sweetest ways,
Folks even your folks would be happy to know.
Though my dreams seem quite improbable
I have a faith that is blind,
For I don't want to go on being lonely
With a dream that is in my mind.

Cinderella One day it will happen, Buttons.

Buttons I'm sure it will, Cinders. (*He hugs her*)

The Baron, Sam, Jack, Mrs Da Palma and the sisters enter

Baron Cinderella! (*He sees the hug*) Oh.

Cinderella It's all right, Father.

Buttons Worse luck.

Baron There's going to be a ball at the palace!

Cinderella What?

Baron It'll be like Monte Carlo.

Mrs Da Palma Don't pretend you've been there.

Cloaca And they say the Prince might choose a person to fall in love with.

Cinderella Oh!

Lymphida He will, he will, me!

Cloaca Fond of vomit, is he?

Lymphida I shall look lovely and glamorous and smell all chemical.

Buttons Miss Harpic of the Year.

Baron There are invitations for everyone, including Cinderella.

Cinderella Me?

Sisters Her?

Sam |
Jack | (*together*) Yes.

Buttons You see?

Cinderella Oh! But I haven't got a dress.

Baron I'll get you one.

Mrs Da Palma Oh—don't you bother, George. I'll get one.

Sisters You will?

Mrs Da Palma Of course. I love her in my way, don't I.

Jack We'll hold you to that.

Buttons It's your dream coming true, Cinders.

Cinderella Is it?

Buttons Of course it is. And I expect the Prince will fall in love with you as madly as anything, bother him.

Lymphida He won't.

Cloaca I'll kill him if he does.

Lymphida Mam, don't let him.

Mrs Da Palma It'll be lovely to have you with us my dear, though of course you'll have to do the chores first, and see to our dresses and do our hair, but if you do all that and one or two other things I'll dream up in the meantime, it'll be lovely.

Cinderella It'll be marvellous! Buttons, it'll be marvellous!

Buttons It will!

Baron Here's your invitation, Cinders.

Mrs Da Palma I'll look after that in case she loses it.

Sam ⎞ (*together*) I don't think you should. Er—just a minute ...
Jack ⎠   *etc.*

Mrs Da Palma It'll be quite safe.

Cinderella Is there one for Buttons?

Jack Oh, well, actually, it's not for people like him, I mean you know, servants.

Lymphida She's a servant.

Sam Inside she's a lady.

Buttons And inside, I'm just Buttons.

Cinderella Oh, Buttons!

Buttons I'll be quite happy sitting at home broken-hearted and playing patience.

Sam Oh, Buttons! You're so understanding.

Cinderella Yes, he is.

Jack And we'll see you all next Tuesday at the ball, including Cinderella.

All Including Cinderella.

Cinderella Including *me*!

Buttons But not me.

SCENE 10

Frontcloth

Sam and Jack and Buttons

Sam Oh, Buttons!

Buttons Yes?

Sam Never mind, Buttons.

Buttons No.

Sam We've got two more invitations for a Nice Little Boy and a Nice Little Girl and you can help us choose them to go instead of you.

Buttons Thank you.

Jack Let's have a look for them.

Buttons All right. There's a nice little boy, lucky thing.

Jack And here's a nice little girl.

Sam And what's your name, nice little girl? And what's your name, nice little boy?

Jack My name's Jack.

Sam And mine—mine's Samantha.

Buttons Samantha? What a surprise.

Sam D'you like it?

Buttons Yes. Quite.

Sam I like Buttons, quite, too.

Jack Let's see if these people are suitable to go to the ball, shall we? Buttons, teach them how to bow.

Buttons Yes. Right, this is how you do the bowing.

Sam I can teach her how to do the curtsying. Lovely.

Buttons And then there's the dancing. Sam and Jack will show you what to do. Can we have a touch of tune, please?

The dance happens

Sam Right, now, hang on to your invitations and when we get the ball, after the interval, we'll come and get you and you can have a lovely time with all the Royals and people. In the meantime——

Mrs Da Palma (*off*) Are there some troublemakers out there?

Buttons No, no-one here. Quick.

Mrs Da Palma (*off*) If there are, they're going in the cupboard.

Buttons No, it's all right. Get back to your seats.

Jack 'Bye, see you later.

Sam 'Bye, Buttons.

Buttons 'Bye. She is quite nice, isn't she? Considering.

They exit

SCENE 11

The Jones's kitchen

Cloaca and Lymphida are being dressed for the ball by Cinderella

Cloaca It's next Tuesday at last! Do my corset up, Cinderella.

Lymphida I haven't been sick for three days. Oh, I'm going to get the Prince.

Cloaca I'm going to get the Prince.

Lymphida I'm going to get the Prince, round the neck if I have to. Do my hair, Cinderella.

Cinderella Coming.

Lymphida And where's my box of tissues?
Cloaca What d'you want them for?
Lymphida In case I want to blow my nose.
Cloaca Just pick it. No-one'll notice.
Lymphida Won't they?
Cloaca No. Royals do it all the time.
Lymphida Oh!

Mrs Da Palma enters in her dress

Mrs Da Palma Straighten my dress, Cinderella.
Cinderella Coming.
Cloaca And do mine up so it flatters.

The three stand in a row

Mrs Da Palma We'll be the belles of the ball with no-one to match us. (*She waves to an imaginary crowd*) Dear people, so nice, and Your Gorgeous Highness, how d'you do.
Lymphida Mam?
Mrs Da Palma Listen to the crowds cheering, "God bless you ma'am". My people, my little folk who love me here on the palace balcony, the lovely Prince beside me on my arm.
Cloaca It's us he's going to marry, Mam.
Mrs Da Palma What? Oh yes, of course, unless he hankers for experience.
Cinderella There. Where's my invitation?
Mrs Da Palma Well, where's your dress?
Cinderella You said you'd get one for me.
Mrs Da Palma Your father said he'd get one. George!

The Baron enters with Buttons

Baron Don't fuss, Buttons.
Cinderella Where's my new dress?
Baron (*to Mrs Da Palma*) You said you'd get one.
Mrs Da Palma Not me.
Baron You did.
Mrs Da Palma Perhaps you have an old one, my dear.
Cinderella You know I haven't. I sold them all to pay for Mother's medicines.
Cloaca You should've thought of that, shouldn't you.
Lymphida It's a real waste of time, buying medicines for someone who's dying.
Mrs Da Palma So. If you haven't got a dress, you won't be able to go to the ball. (*She tears up the invitation*) Dear me.
Cinderella But you promised! Father?
Baron I'm so sorry.
Cinderella Sorry?
Baron What else can I be?
Mrs Da Palma You must speak to her about her temper, George. Have our cocoa ready for us when we get back.

She sweeps out with the Baron

Lymphida We'll be tired out, dancing with the Prince.
Cloaca Try biting your nails while your doing that, Lymphida, he'll love it.

Cloaca and Lymphida exit

Cinderella You've let me down! I've done everything all of you asked, and now ... Oh, I hate you all! (*She cries*)
Buttons You swine! You worse than swine—you utter swine! If I had the key to that cupboard, I'd lock you in it, and throw it in the river and torpedo it, and then pour tons of concrete on it, and drop a bomb on it, and set a lot of sharks at it and big green slimey octopuses, and then boil it so you came out pink like lobsters, and I'd eat you up with those long prongy forks, and then I'd do what Lymphida does, and flush you into the nastiest sewage works in the world. Then I'd gob at you. Poor Cinders, try to cheer up. (*He hugs her*)
Cinderella What's the use of cheering up? There's nothing we can do.
Buttons There's always something we can do.
Cinderella My step-mother must be right. I'm just not nice enough to have good things happen to me.
Buttons (*suddenly seized*) Oh—oh—there's something deep down talking to me. The Fairy Godmother. Shout.

All shout "Fairy Godmother, Fairy Godmother"

A huge flash and the Fairy Godmother appears very excited

Fairy Godmother This is it! This is the Big One! Haha! I can let rip with a real corker now! Oh yes! Gung ho! Cinderella, my dear, lovable Cinderella, you *shall* go to the ball!
Cinderella That cloak—who are you?
Fairy Godmother Your Fairy Godmother, and I'm fearfully over-excited. Have you got a spare pumpkin?
Buttons (*dashing around for it*) Yes! Yes, I have. I bought Cinderella one ages ago—I knew it would be useful.
Fairy Godmother Just stop staring and get it, will you dear.
Cinderella What? Oh yes.

Cinderella runs off

Fairy Godmother And some dead rats?
Buttons I'll get those. The place is full of them. I used to know this one as a matter of fact, Oswald the terror of the cheese cupboard, ate a cat for breakfast every day, ruled the larder with a claw of iron. Alas, poor Oswald, has it come to this?
Fairy Godmother And some lizards.
Buttons Lizards. Lizards, lizards.
Fairy Godmother Where's that pumpkin then?
Cinderella (*off*) Here.

Cinderella substitute brings it on

Fairy Godmother It's the moment of moments. This is the night we beat those harpies at their own game, because we are all very sweet and very lovely and they are absolutely ghastly. Now stand still. Virtue is going to be rewarded!

Music. Lights. Thunder. Amazement. Transformation. A coach and four horses. These are the same sort of horses as we have seen. Four members of the company wearing turbans and half-masks are operating them so they look like exotic riders. Cinderella is in a lovely gown. Buttons has a powdered wig on

Buttons Oh Cinders, you look absolutely smashing.
Cinderella Do I? If only Mother could see me now.
Fairy Godmother This isn't a wake, it's a ball, and here's your invitation. Young man, you can go as her footman.
Buttons (*of his wig*) Oh, look, a dead seagull.
Fairy Godmother There's this one warning. Since I've spent my entire allocation of magic doing this remarkable thing, I can't do anything else for you. Furthermore, I can't stretch my spell any further than this evening, so you must leave the ball at midnight.
Cinderella } (*together*) Midnight?
Buttons
Fairy Godmother When midnight strikes you will turn back into a skivvy, and that will be your lot.
Buttons Oh dear.
Fairy Godmother Well, times are hard. Now enjoy yourself and be a princess for the evening.

Song 10: Simple Cinders, Delicious Girl

(*Singing*)   Simple Cinders, delicious girl,
Soft of cheek and beguiling curl.
All your sweetness and loveliness
Stands revealed in your well-cut dress.
Now you look what you really are,
Moon of moons and of stars the star.
Lesser mortals you'll sweep aside,
Father's joy and a mother's pride.

With Chorus and probably Cinderella and Buttons ...

All the world she will take by storm
In her new fully-fashioned form,
Gliding over the ballroom floor,
Humbly watching the crowds adore,
She will blush as the angels sing
"What a catch for a future king."
Love will come in a sweeping tide,
Father's joy and a mother's pride.

The coach moves off, Buttons as postillion

Fairy Godmother (*speaking*) That should spoil it for the Da Palma sisters. Let's all go and have an ice-cream to celebrate.

CURTAIN

ACT II

SCENE 1

Prelude before frontcloth

Sam and Jack enter

Sam Where are those two nice little people? There. Ready for the ball?

Jack Here are your clothes. And a lovely wig for the nice little boy.

Sam And I've got one for the nice little girl. So there we are, full of biff and bim.

Jack Right, then, let's got to the ball, shall we? No sign of that silly friend of yours.

And the frontcloth rises

Sam He wasn't invited, was he?

SCENE 2

The ballroom at the palace

Everything is very crystal. The whole cast is present except for Cinderella, Buttons and the Fairy Godmother. They are all dancing a veleta waltz

Song 11: The Schmaltz Waltz

All	All here at the ball Ah-ha! The long, the short and the tall Ah-ha! All trying to be Careless, easy and free.
Girls	None lets it be seen Ah-ha She wants to be queen. Ah-ha We're all being so Very cool, *comme il faut* As we waltz to the schmaltz Of the ball.
Men	All eyes on the Prince. Ah-ha

          Has he dropped any hints?
          Ah-ha
King   He seems to have got
          A rather second-rate lot.
Prince   What gives me a thrill
          Ah-ha
          Though they're run of the mill
          Ah-ha
          Is just the fun of
          Being guest Number One
          As we waltz to the schmaltz of the ball.

They all continue the stately veleta. The Prince is dancing with Lymphida, quite close to where Cloaca is dancing with someone else

Lymphida What are these, Your Highness?
Cloaca (*in a loud whisper*) Nails, Lymph.
Lymphida What? Oh yes. (*She bites her nails while grinning at the Prince*)
Prince They're medals for being brave and that.
Cloaca (*in a loud whisper*) Nose, Lymph, nose.
Lymphida All *right*! (*She sticks her finger up her nose*) Are you very brave, then?
Prince Yes, especially at the moment.
Lymphida What d'you mean, especially at the moment? Mam, what does he mean, Mam?
Mrs Da Palma (*of her finger*) For goodness' sake pull that thing out. (*To Cloaca*) Did you put her up to that?
Cloaca No.
Lymphida (*of her finger*) It's stuck.
Cloaca Put some butter up your nostril, then. (*Replacing her as the Prince's partner*) Hallo, I'm the clever sister. Just what's needed by the throne, eh? Subtlety, wisdom, insight?
Prince Isn't there another one?
Sam ⎫
Jack ⎬ (*together*) Yes!
Mrs Da Palma No!
Prince A grubby one.
Baron She's lovely and she's kind and she's——

Mrs Da Palma kicks him

    Ow! I'm nice, I'm nice, I'm sorry and I'm nice.
Queen Don't be sorry, Baron. I'm nice, too, and so is James, and we're helpless in each other's arms.
King How deliciously improper.
Queen (*abandoned*) It is, it is.
Mrs Da Palma (*of Lymphida's finger, now free*) That's it. Now wipe it on your skirt.

As the dance continues they all start to sing again

All	Lost high in the clouds
	Aha
	Dancing gently in crowds
	Aha
	How graceful we seem,
	A sweet midsummer night's dream.
Girls	Look under our wigs
	Aha
	We're really greedy as pigs
	Aha
	For each has a yen
	To be his favourite hen
	As we waltz to the schmaltz of the ball.

The dance ends. The children incidentally will have been dancing with Sam and Jack. Everyone bows and curtsies

Queen Enjoy yourselves everyone, while I cuddle with the King.
King Charlotte!
Sam (*to Lymphida*) Where's Cinderella?
Lymphida She's been left behind because we hate her.
Jack You broke your word.
Lymphida Yes!
Sam Right, you'll pay for this.
Jack You two, come here.

They walk to the two children

Cloaca I'm afraid my sister has more bogies under her finger-nails than you've had hot dinners, Your Highness.
Lymphida It's me who was dancing with him, Cloaca, so come here.
Cloaca Pooh.
Lymphida Cloaca!

She moves forward to Cloaca but the children, under instructions from Sam and Jack, stand on her dress. It tears

Aaaah!
Mrs Da Palma Who did that?
Jack A nail.
Sam A large nail.
Lymphida Mam, me bum!
Mrs Da Palma It was done by troublemakers. Those troublemakers.
Sam They're Royal Cousins, aren't they Jack?
Jack Yes.
King What?
Jack We seem to be telling a lot of fibs.
Lymphida Put them in the cupboard, Mam, and feed them on cockroaches.
King You can't feed Royal Cousins on cockroaches. Stop her.
Sam Don't you come near them.

Sudden trumpets

King Oh heavens, even on the dance floor!

The glamorous Buttons enters

Buttons Ladies and gentlemen! Pray silence for Her Royal Highness, the Mysterious Princess Most Beautiful of All.

More trumpets for the entry of the lovely Cinderella

All are amazed but the Prince, who is being forcibly detained by Cloaca

Queen Oh Hugo, she's absolutely incredible.

King Unbelievable.

Mrs Da Palma Who is it, blast it?

Jack I don't know.

Baron She's more lovely than I could've imagined.

Cinderella Your Royal Highness?

Prince Someone's standing on my foot.

Cinderella (*gentle but firm*) Well, push her off. We can't wait all night to meet each other, can we?

Prince (*getting free*) Pardon? (*He sees her*) Oh, my goodness.

Cinderella How lovely to see you again. And how charming the palace is, once you get inside it.

Prince I didn't know anyone could be as beautiful as you.

Cloaca Mam, he's going to fall in love.

Lymphida Mam, he is.

Queen I hope so.

Mrs Da Palma Not if I can help it, and cover your smalls. (*To the audience*) Don't look, so rude.

Prince I don't remember inviting you, though I can't think how I could forget.

Cinderella You did invite me, Your Highness, and I'd like to say that you're much more handsome than I remember.

Prince Where've I seen you before, then?

Buttons A mind like a sieve. It's just the way he dresses that impresses.

Prince Is this your boy-friend?

Cinderella Oh no. He's lovely, but he doesn't make me go all funny inside.

Prince Do I?

Cinderella To be honest, Your Highness, yes, you do.

Prince Oh, how wonderful!

Buttons How do people do that, the going all funny inside?

Sam Aaah.

Prince Ladies and gentlemen, I intend to spend the rest of the evening in this lady's company, and it looks as if I will fall in love with her.

King Charlotte, there's hope at last. (*He speaks to the band*)

Lymphida I knew it, I just knew it!

Mrs Da Palma Shut up and try to look adult.

Lymphida What?

Mrs Da Palma I've got to think.

Cinderella Buttons, I think this is it.

Buttons Before you decide anything, just remember there's a humble but honest heart beneath this wig that beats in loyalty only to you.
Cinderella This is something beyond loyalty.
Buttons There's nothing beyond loyalty.
Cinderella There's white-hot burning passion, and that's what I've got.
Buttons Oh, bother! I'm so happy of course, but bother, bother, bother.
Sam Can I help you?
Buttons Not really.
Jack (*to Sam*) Do remember who you are, Sam.
Mrs Da Palma Cloaca, dance with George here, and make it an excuse me.
King The floor is for the Prince and Princess only, madam.
Cloaca Who says so?
King Me.
Queen And he's king.

Song 12: Paradise

Prince

I never used to notice Spring and things,
Or the darling buds of May.
I never thought of wedding rings
But all that was yesterday.
For suddenly a wonder is standing there
And I'm freshly minted anew.
Now I know that I simply cannot bear
To be away from you.
I'm in Paradise
Simply Paradise.
No-one ever touched my heart with love
                               like this,
And I tell you the experience is bliss,
As I step out as I never stepped
                               before.

Cinderella

No-one told me I
Could feel quite so high
In the arms of someone I once thought
                               a fool,
And who sparkles in my heart now like a
                               jewel,

Both As we dance alone in love across the floor.

Prince (*middle eight*)

Once I felt
Nothing but boredom,
Always-want-more-dom,
Surrounded by friends.

Cinderella

Now I know
Love is a two-some
A me-and-you-some,
Which never ends.

Return to tune

Both
It is a joy to be
Simply you and me
With this unexpected, unaffected score,
Which we'll have them play for us for
ever more,
As we dance alone in love across the
floor.

Big dance break for Prince and Cinderella. Then ...

All (*except the sisters*)
They're in Paradise
It's extremely nice,
We have never seen a love that looks
like that.
You may think it all remarkable old hat,
But they clearly feel things they've
not felt before.

Sisters
It's an awful frost.
We're afraid we've lost.
We're so angry we could stamp our feet
and weep,
And though beauty, it is true, is just
skin deep,
There's a lot of skin there dancing on
the floor.

All (*middle eight*)
They're in love,
Nothing can budge them,
Fudge them or mudge them,
They're under a spell.
Everything's
Coming up roses,
Sweet to our noses,
Fragrant the smell.

They are so in love,
Truly hand in glove,
They are hearing sounds they've
never heard before,
It's a true romance for them you can
be sure,
As they dance alone in love

Prince
Cinderella   } We ride the stars above
All   As they dance alone in love across
the floor!

The dance ends and the two lovers stand C facing each other

Cinderella Oh that was wonderful.

Prince But you are wonderful.

Cinderella When you say it, I think I just might be.

King Is this it then, Hugo?

Prince I think so, Father.

Queen There'll be grandchildren!

King Wonderful!

Cloaca She's mutton dressed as lamb in my opinion.

Cinderella What?

Lymphida Not the real thing at all.

Cinderella And who are you?

Buttons They're said to be Baron Jones's step-daughters, but if you ask me they're just a pair of pick-pockets on the look out for a loose tiara.

Cloaca We're first-rate girls with a very good family history.

Lymphida Mam wrote it for us.

Mrs Da Palma Ahaha, their little joke, so witty. Between you and me, you'd be throwing yourself away on Prince Hugo, my dear. Tatty little kingdom, no decent people to talk to—do us all a favour and buzz off.

Cinderella No, certainly not, I've fallen in love.

Mrs Da Palma What's it worth to you to fall out again?

Cinderella I don't want money, thank you. And your daughter's going to be sick if she eats as fast as that.

Lymphida Everyone's always at me.

Baron I'm Baron Jones, Your Highness.

Buttons A simple man, but well meaning.

Baron Who told you that?

Buttons A clever young person of great good looks called Boutons.

Baron Boutons?

Cinderella They say you are a very loving father, Baron.

Baron Oh I am, I am, but somehow useless.

Buttons Helpless.

Baron Thoughtless.

Buttons Brainless.

Baron You understand people very clearly, don't you?

Buttons Yes.

Prince Please come and meet my parents, the King and Queen.

Cinderella Coming, Hugo.

Mrs Da Palma Hugo?

Baron Oh well, perhaps I'll meet her again.

Buttons I'm sure you will, *mon brave*.

Cloaca Go on, Mam, think of something, like poison in her caviare.

A clock begins to strike

Buttons Oh goodness, the time. (*To the kids*) You two, I can't get to her. Quick, tell her it's nearly midnight and that if she stays the magic will wear off. I've got to get the coach.

The children rush to Cinderella. They point to the clock

Sam What is it? What's happening?

Cinderella What? Oh, midnight! I'll change back to my grubby old self! Your Highness, excuse me, and please, don't forget me.

She rushes off, leaving behind a slipper

Prince Stop her. Find her. I don't even know her name.

King Yes, stop her. Arrest her if you have to.

Lymphida Let her go.

Queen No. We can't have everything unsettled all over again.

Mrs Da Palma She's a fraud, that's what, upwardly mobile in that nasty way people have. Forget her, Your Highness, and go for girls of solid worth.

Sisters Us.

Prince But I love her. I want to marry her.

Mrs Da Palma No, you don't. Forget her, forget her, forget her. She's deceived you.

At this moment the humble Cinderella rushes across the back of the stage in her rags

She is seen only by the King, Queen and Prince

King Who on earth's that?

Prince A beggar in the palace?

Baron Where?

Mrs Da Palma Where?

Queen I hope she had some food.

The Prince picks up the slipper that Cinderella has left behind

Prince Look, a shoe. It's one she was wearing when she danced with me.

King Oh, well, that's easy! I'll make a proclamation.

Queen Really James? After all these years?

King I shall make a proclamation for everyone to come for a shoe fitting. Hugo's very upset and I'm not going on with this job a moment longer than I have to.

Mrs Da Palma Girls this is our chance! Trust your mother to get your Prince for you.

Song 13: Proclamation

King	Here is the shoe,
	And this is what we'll do;
	We'll find the foot that fits it
	Neat and snugly, tight and true.
	Thus we will know
	From some exquisite toe,
	Who's unsettled Hugo
	And has overturned him so.
Prince	I'll marry her!
Others	He'll marry her!

Prince	Whoever fits this shoe shall be my wife!
	I will search through all the city
	For a girl who's young and pretty
	And whose slipper makes her mine for all
	my life.

Song 14: The Dancer I'll Love

Prince	For I love the girl
	With the slipper so small,
	With the step so firm,
	And the head held high,
	And I promise the world
	I will give my all
	To the dancer I'll love
	Till the day that I die.
	I love the girl
	With the swinging young hair,
	And the lips so warm,
	And the laughing eye,
	And nothing will change
	In my love affair
	For the dancer I'll love
	Till the day that I die.
	She danced my heart
	Away from me.
	And took control
	Of my destiny,
	And until I find her
	My heart will cry
	For the dancer I'll love
	Till the day that I die.

Repeat lines 1–8, followed by lines 17–24

King That's more or less what I was going to say, Charlotte.

Mrs Da Palma The slipper, girls. Your feet will fit that slipper, girls, come what may.

Baron The surgeon's knife will have to come in that case.

All but the Prince exit

Prince (*reprise*)	For I love the girl
	With the slipper so small
	With the step so firm,
	And the head held high,
	And I promise the world
	I will give my all
	To the dancer I'll love
	Till the day that I die.

SCENE 3

Frontcloth

Sam and Jack come forward with the two children from the audience

Sam Actually, (*boy's name*) and (*girl's name*) have told us who the mysterious Princess is.

Jack They say it's (*he whispers*) Cinderella. Are they right? Then all we have to do is tell the Prince and that will be that. Give us your gowns and wigs.

Sam They also say that lovely footman was really Buttons.

Jack Are you going completely sloppy, Sam?

Sam My name's Samantha.

Jack Pull yourself together. Help me get these nice people back into the audience.

The children return to their seats

Then we can go to the Prince and tell him—oh.

Mrs Da Palma enters

Mrs Da Palma Tell him what?

Jack Er—er . . .

Sam Nothing really, absolutely nothing, really.

Mrs Da Palma Oh really? Nothing really?

Jack Absolutely and completely nothing really.

Mrs Da Palma Here am I, waiting to go home from the ball, when I hear muttering, and muttering always seems to mean you two talking to those troublemakers out there, two of whom, I see, are what you call Royal Cousins.

Jack No, no, they're not, they're quite different.

Sam They just happen to look the same.

Mrs Da Palma They're going in my cupboard when I get the chance and I'll pull the dreaded silence lever so they can't be heard, because they're troublemakers—the whole world seems full of troublemakers, all of whom are trying to stop one of my daughters marrying the Prince. And if I hear any whispering, or plotting, or planning or anything remotely suspicious in any way whatsoever, the first thing I will do is put Buttons, and Cinderella, and the Baron, into my cupboard, because I know you'd all hate that, so you've been warned. I'm in charge. Just understand that.

Lymphida (*off*) Ma-a-am!

Mrs Da Palma Coming, my innocent little leech.

She goes

Jack We'd better say nothing for the moment.

Sam I certainly don't want that lovely Buttons going in the cupboard.

Jack It's Cinderella I'm worried about. One thing's for sure. I don't know what we're going to do next.

They exit

Scene 4

The Jones's kitchen, after midnight

It is empty

Into it burst Cinderella and Buttons in their normal clothes

Buttons Hallo, Fairy Godmother! Fairy Godmother! She's gone.

Cinderella Everything's gone. It was another horrible joke, wasn't it, like that woman promising me a dress.

Buttons No, it wasn't.

Cinderella Yes, it was.

Buttons The Prince loved you.

Cinderella I loved him but he saw me in my real clothes and he called me a beggar.

The Fairy Godmother enters

Fairy Godmother Some of my best friend are beggars. They're often nicer that way than the other.

Cinderella Thank heavens you've come.

Fairy Godmother I'm only passing.

Buttons We're in a terrible mess because we stayed too long.

Fairy Godmother Of course you did.

Cinderella Why did you let him see me as I am?

Fairy Godmother Because what you are is what he loves. What did you do with the slipper?

Buttons What slipper?

Cinderella What slipper?

Fairy Godmother Oh come on. Only one slipper was returned to the magic wardrobe. What happened to the other?

Cinderella It fell off.

Buttons Ooh! You minx.

Fairy Godmother No, no, no. She was being perfectly sensible. Now he'll be able to find her, if he has any brain at all, and when he does, he'll find her precisely as she is.

Cinderella A mess. I even smell a bit.

Fairy Godmother If he's in love with you that is precisely what will catch him. People love each other's natural perfumes, don't they, Buttons?

Cinderella Really?

Buttons Oh yes, let me tell you . . .

Song 15: Don't Wash, My Darling

(Singing)   You're wretched rough and ragged,
Your hair's alive with nits,
Your only dress is such a mess
That it falls into bits.
Yet if your Prince adores you
It's for yourself alone,

So it's quite likely he will cry
While making you his own—

Chorus

Buttons Oh—

Fairy Godmother Don't wash my darling,
I love the way you pong.
You may not smell of the best Chanel—
It's you, though, good and strong.
I love you for the way you are
And not because you're posh,
So give me hope, throw out your soap,
And please—don't—wash.

Buttons Your knees could well be lumpy,
From scrubbing of the floors,
Your elbows look like marrows and
Your shoulders broad as doors.
Your broken nails and horny hands
May speak of sweaty toil,
But if he loves you, he will cry
When coming to the boil—

Buttons Oh—

Fairy Godmother Don't wash, my darling,
I love the way you pong,
You may not smell of the best Chanel—
It's you, though, good and strong.
I love you for the way you are
And not because you're posh,
So give me hope, throw out your soap,
And please—don't—wash.
Don't wash!

Cinderella Are you sure about this?

Buttons Absolutely.

Fairy Godmother So stop moaning, be yourself, show him what you're made of and I'll be back later to see how you're getting on.

A flash and she's gone

Cinderella You see? She's gone and left me alone again, let me down, as always.

Buttons You do say that a lot.

Cinderella It helps if you blame other people.

Buttons Well, I have a very difficult part in this story and it would help me if you stopped doing it.

Cinderella Don't talk like that, Buttons. You're supposed to give me comfort.

The Da Palmas and the Baron burst in

Cloaca It's us who need comfort. What an awful evening.

Lymphida My dress got torn and the Prince fell in love with someone else.

Cinderella Fell in love?
Buttons How d'you know?
Cloaca He said so, stupid.
Cinderella He said so?
Mrs Da Palma Over and over, the boring little potentate.
Cinderella What was she like, Father, this other person?
Baron Utterly beautiful. Absolutely, utterly.
Lymphida She told me how to eat my food so I wouldn't throw up.
Cloaca She muscled in on me with the Prince.
Mrs Da Palma She was someone we wouldn't ever want to meet again.
Baron Well, I would. She said I was a very loving man.
Mrs Da Palma Exactly. She was naïve.
Lymphida The thing is, she left her slipper behind, and the Prince says he's going to marry whoever it fits.
Buttons Oh really, how interesting, well, well.
Cinderella (*excited*) How marvellous, Buttons.
Cloaca Funnily enough, it looks as if it might fit me.
Lymphida Oooh, it never. Much more like me.
Buttons Don't be silly.
Mrs Da Palma What do you know about it?
Baron It might fit Cinderella, actually.
All Da Palmas What!?
Cloaca Put him in the cupboard, Mother.
Lymphida Yes, in the cupboard.
Mrs Da Palma You're saying things that aren't nice again and we don't want that.
Baron Oh please, not the cupboard.
Lymphida Yes, the cupboard, while we think how to make our feet the right size for the Prince.
Mrs Da Palma And that goes for anyone else who behaves suspiciously, or rocks the boat, or puts a spanner in the works, or in any way threatens to pull the plug on my two luscious little birds of paradise. Understood? Get him upstairs.

The Baron, Mrs Da Palma and the sisters leave

Buttons Leave the poor old boy alone! He doesn't like the cupboard. Let him be!
Cinderella Oh—it would be simplest if one of them married Hugo and we all just went on as usual.
Buttons Simplest, but not best. You love him, he loves you, they're pigs and they need putting out in the sty. We've got to do it, somehow, Cinders. Now get some sleep while I sit here and keep watch over you.
Cinderella Faithful Buttons.
Buttons Yes, well if you're not good at making people go funny inside, faithful is what you do instead. Off you go, snoozey woozey. That's my girl. (*He here sings a reprise of "The Dancer I Love"*)

Song 14: The Dancer I Love (Reprise)

(Singing)   She stole my heart
                       Away from me
                       And took control
                       Of my destiny,
                       And until I find her
                       My heart will cry
                       For the dancer I love
                       Till the day that I die.
                       For I love the girl
                       With the slipper so small,
                       With the step so firm,
                       And the head held high.
                       And I promise the world
                       I will give my all
                       To the dancer I'll love
                       Till the day that I die.

SCENE 5

The throne room

The King and Queen are asleep on the steps

The Prince enters

Prince Mother, Father, Sam, Jack. Shoe-fitting time. Come on. Good heavens, this place is half asleep.

King What on earth is it?

Queen We were awake half the night.

Prince We have to move quickly because she might have to go somewhere and we'll miss her. Samantha! Jack! Wake up!

Queen He's worse when he's doing something than when he's doing nothing.

King We don't know anyone called Samantha, do we?

Sam and Jack enter

Jack Here we are, Hugo.

Sam Ready Hugo.

Queen It's that one.

King Oh, it's changed its name, has it?

Prince Now, here's the slipper, and there's masses of people out there (*the audience*) and whoever fits this shoe I will marry.

All Ah!

Prince You don't have to try every foot of course. Some are obviously wrong—yours Sam, feet like hippos, I've seen them, and (*to the Queen*) of course, you're my mother.

Jack (*to Sam*) Suppose he gets the wrong one?

Sam He won't.

Jack We'll have to make sure.

Sam We just go along with him and eventually we'll get to Cinderella and that will be lovely.

King Is she still a girl, or has she changed that, as well?

Prince Rally round, everyone.

Song 16: Come All Ye Well-shod Girls

(*Singing*)   Come all you well-shod girls of every
                                                    size,
             Take off your sandals, your boots and
                                                    shoes,
             The day when love has opened wide his
                                                    eyes
             Must end with one foot that he must
                                                    choose.
             Show your corns, veruccas and your
                                                    bunions,
             Your carbuncles, big and hard as rocks,
             Bare your soles, stocking holes, don't
                                                    be shy!
             Never mind the lumps big as onions,
             Nor even the smell of your socks.
             Throw off, your modesty!
             Reveal the hosiery
             Try on! Try on! Shyness be gone!
             Unshoe, and let us see!

They go into the audience and we hear things like the following

All (*variously*) This one might do. No, too big.
             No, too small.
             Pooh, the stink. Don't they have
             baths out there in the world?
             This one's it.
             No, it isn't Buttons. (*Quite often*)
             There are things on this foot like
             pickled walnuts/hard-boiled eggs/
             rotten apples/old rugger balls/
             stalagmites/thirteen toes.

King and **Queen** This one's a real sweetie, a real darling, wrong size of foot but every inch a princess ... (*etc*).

Prince I refuse to marry her, even if it does fit, she's too old, ugly, like my maiden aunt, bossy-looking, red-haired ... (*etc*).

Others But you promised, but you said, but you can't go back on your word ... *etc*. Anyway it doesn't fit so that's that.

Finally, they return to the stage

Prince Obviously it's no-one there.
King We haven't tried everyone yet.
Jack You can tell, though, at a glance.
Prince And I know a thoroughbred when I see one.
Sam We'll have to go out into the Kingdom, Hugo.
Prince Yes, we will. This way.

Mrs Da Palma enters in disguise

Prince Oh, who are you?
Mrs Da Palma I'm one of the Less Fortunate, Your Highness.
Prince I'm past all that, I'm afraid.
Mrs Da Palma And I just thought I could try on the slipper.
Prince You? Don't be silly. The wearer of this slipper was a lady.
Queen Let her look at it, Hugo.
Prince Here it is, then. Look.
Mrs Da Palma Size six, I think. Thank you, Your Highness. I'll never forget
    you.
Jack I know that voice.

Mrs Da Palma is heading for the audience

Prince Where are you going?
Mrs Da Palma There are two people down there I want to show a cupboard
    to.
King A cupboard?
Sam Jack, Jack, quick.
Jack I know who you are.
Sam And so do I.
Mrs Da Palma I'm an old lady of the road, and you will never see your
    friends again if you say different.
Prince This is the way out, madam, not that . . .
Mrs Da Palma (*returning from the audience*) Oh thank you, sire. (*To the two
    kids in the audience*) I haven't forgotten you.

She goes

Queen What was that about a cupboard?
King Was she giving her poor doggie a bone, or what?
Prince Stop fussing and let's get out into the highways and byways and try
    this shoe on all the likely young feet there are. Father, start ruling
    properly. There are at least two bridges waiting to be opened.

He goes out with the slipper

King Oh, I like opening bridges. I'll get my scissors.
Queen It's you who's got to start ruling, Hugo! We're giving up!
Jack That woman's going to do something awful. I know it.

The King and Queen exit

SCENE 6

Frontcloth

Sam and Jack

Sam She's going to put my Buttons in a box and suffocate him.
Jack Probably.
Sam I can't think of anything but Buttons, Buttons, Buttons, Buttons——
Aaah!

Buttons walks on

Buttons Have you seen Mrs Da Palma?
Jack She was here just now, getting the size of the slipper.
Sam Oh Buttons, you're safe, darling Buttons, I've been so frightened
because Mrs Da Palma's going to put you in a cupboard, and all of them
in a cupboard, and everybody in a cupboard and oh, Buttons, Buttons,
Buttons, oh Buttons.
Buttons Are you all funny inside?
Sam Yes.
Jack Yes, she is. It's a bit embarrassing.
Buttons It's marvellous. I've done it at last. Don't you worry Samantha, I'll
save the day.
Jack A footman?
Sam Oh, Buttons.
Buttons As I was keeping watch over Cinderella——
Jack The Prince's true love . . .
Buttons —I saw Mrs Da Palma creeping out and I followed her here, sleuth-
like and undetected. I now realize that she is going to arrange for her
daughter's feet to be made the right size for the famous slipper.
Sam Oh Buttons, how clever you are. What shall we do?
Buttons We shall thwart her.
Sam Of course.
Jack How??
Buttons Ah. Um. Ho.
Sam Magic? We've had some magic, perhaps we could have some more.
Buttons It's not allowed. What we'll have is B.G.P.
Jack B.G.P.?
Buttons Boy and Girl Power . . . Just look out there, all that wondrous great
crowd of troublemakers.
Jack What use will they be?
Buttons Why, we'll teach them a song of course. We'll teach them this song.

A song sheet comes down

Song 17: Shout, Shout, Shout

(Singing)   If you want to be a happy fella
                     Shout, shout, shout, for Cinderella

> She's got the feet
> That are pretty and petite
> So shout, shout, shout, for Cinderella

Business

(*Speaking*) Marvellous.
Sam Terriff.
Jack Really very good indeed.
Buttons So at the Right Moment, we'll get them to sing this song. OK?
Jack At the Right Moment.
Sam The Right Moment.
Buttons And in the meantime, I'll go home and pretend to do everything I'm asked by Mrs Da Palma.
Sam Oh, Buttons! Take care.
Buttons Oh, Samantha! Be brave.

They gaze at each other

Marvellous isn't it. All funny inside.

He goes

Sam Jack, I'm going to faint.
Jack Love strikes me as very boring.

They exit

Scene 7

A bedroom in the Baron's house

The cupboard is there. The Baron is heard to be in it when he speaks. At the moment, only Cloaca and Lymphida are in the room

Baron (*from the cupboard*) Can I come out now?
Cloaca Not until you promise to keep quiet when the Prince comes.
Lymphida Mam, where are you?

Mrs Da Palma enters with Buttons, carrying a tool bag

Mrs Da Palma Here I am, my chickens.
Lymphida Have you found the shoe size?
Mrs Da Palma Yes.
Buttons Who's in there?
Cloaca Baron Boney Bonce.
Buttons But he's been there all night.
Mrs Da Palma Are you nice yet, George?
Baron Ever so nice, Joy.
Mrs Da Palma Are you going to tell the Prince you have a grubby daughter with small feet?
Baron I might.

Mrs Da Palma That's not nice, George. Pull the——

Baron No Joy, no, you can't do that. Joy, please don't pull——

Silence as the lever is pulled

Buttons That's awful! Baron!

Mrs Da Palma He can't hear you, we can't hear him—it's lovely. Want to try it?

Buttons No!

Cloaca The shoe size, Mam, tell us the shoe size.

Mrs Da Palma The shoe size is number six with special fittings. What size do you take, Cloaca?

Cloaca Fourteen.

Lymphida Ahahahahahaha.

Buttons What's so funny, twinkle-toes? What's your size?

Lymphida Four. But I can stuff my socks out with cotton wool.

Mrs Da Palma Never trust in that sort of thing. Sit down here, and hand me a pair of pliers, Buttons.

Buttons The pliers? You aren't going to elongate her toes?

Lymphida Yes, she is, and I want her to, because I want the Prince, so give her the pliers!

Buttons All right. If you say so. (*He hands over the pliers*)

Mrs Da Palma Hold on to her, Buttons.

Buttons She'll scream.

Lymphida Hold me!

Buttons All right.

Cloaca Come on, give us your tiny little tootsies.

Lymphida I might be sick of course.

Buttons Eh?

Cloaca No you won't, because you'll have a lovely long foot to fit the Prince's shoe.

Buttons Are you sure you want this?

Lymphida Yes! I do!

Mrs Da Palma Hold tight. And remember, Lymphida, this hurts me more than it hurts you, because one day you may be Queen and I won't.

Buttons holds the girl and Cloaca and Mrs Da Palma pull on the pliers. Great grunts and groans as the foot grows longer

Buttons You're doing it. She's really doing it!

Mrs Da Palma Hold on, Buttons, they're coming good and long.

Lymphida Oh Mam, it is hurting a bit. Will I really be Queen, Mam?

Mrs Da Palma You won't if you don't try. Pull, Pull, Pull. There!

Lymphida now has a long limp foot

Lymphida Is that going to do?

Mrs Da Palma I hope so.

Buttons Looks like a family of slugs. Do they leave a slimey trail when you walk?

Lymphida My feet always do that.

Buttons Well, the Prince'll really love those.

Lymphida Will he, Mam?

Mrs Da Palma They say he does favour the Less Fortunate. Now, the second string to our bow. Put your foot up, Cloaca. Give me the axe, Buttons.

Buttons Not the axe.

Cloaca Yes, the axe.

Buttons Can you believe it? Major surgery, without an anaesthetic. Remarkable.

Cloaca Come on, get on with it.

Mrs Da Palma You won't feel much, darling girl. And remember, this might make you Queen.

She brings down the axe on Cloaca's toes. Cloaca's mouth falls open in silent pain

Lymphida Oh look, Jacks. (*She picks up the toes and plays jacks with them*)

Cloaca Mam, those are my toes.

Lymphida Not any more.

Buttons Don't mess them about, Lymphida. They'd be nice fried with a few tomatoes.

Lymphida Would they?

Buttons No, come to think of it, they're probably past their sell-by date.

Cloaca (*crying and angry*) I don't mind the pain, but I do mind my toes being played with.

She chases Lymphida off

Mrs Da Palma Grin and bear it dear. And never say I haven't done my best by my family. I've mutilated my children, locked my husband in the cupboard, and turned my step-daughter into a slave. There was, of course, no alternative! (*She pulls the lever*) Are you nice yet, George?

Baron (*from the cupboard*) Yes, nicer than anyone in the world.

Mrs Da Palma Will you keep quiet about Cinderella's feet?

Baron Yes!

Mrs Da Palma Let him out, then Buttons. I've got another use for that. Take it to the kitchen, George.

Baron You're not going to put Cinderella in it.

Mrs Da Palma You said you were nice.

Baron Yes!

Buttons But you can't put Cinderella in——

Mrs Da Palma If you can't be positive, keep quiet. This is a hard world and only certain people can succeed in it.

The rest leave as ...

Mrs Da Palma sings

Song 18: Be A * * *

(*Singing*)   If you want to get ahead,
                         Be a sod,

Overdressed and overfed,
    Be a sod.
If your daughters want a prince
Who'll give them steak and never mince,
Chop their toes off, do not wince,
And be a sod, sod, sod.
And if you want to win the game
    Be a beast,
Do not wilt in guilt and shame,
    Be a beast.
If there's someone in your way
Who moans and groans about fairplay,
Smash his nose in, shout hooray
And be a beast, beast, beast.

Middle eight (over)

Do not dodge the world of battle and of
                 strife here,
That leads to being nothing after all.
If you want to get the best out of your
                 life here,
Give your enemies a call,
And put your boots on and stand tall,
Knock them over, kick their heads in,
Grind their faces very small.
And if you want to get on top
    Be a rat.
If it hurts you mustn't stop,
    Be a rat.
If your children's lives are wrecked,
And friends go off you and defect,
Well, you've still got self-respect
For you're a rat, rat, rat.

Mrs Da Palma exits

SCENE 8

Frontcloth
Buttons rushes on

Buttons You heard what she's going to do, she's going to put Cinderella in that cupboard and then she's going to pull the silencing lever, and it's all going to be terrible, and I can't manage on my own. Fairy Godmother! Fairy Godmother!

The Fairy Godmother appears

Fairy Godmother You've got the right idea with B.G.P.
Buttons Oh?
Fairy Godmother (*to the audience*) Nothing to beat it. You know the song, don't you? Yes. Then listen for the Right Moment, and when it comes, just sing your socks off.
Buttons How will they know when it comes?
Fairy Godmother You'll tell them.
Buttons But how will I know?
Fairy Godmother Don't panic Buttons. You'll recognize it.
Buttons But suppose I don't, and suppose everything goes wrong, and suppose, suppose, suppose, suppose, suppose!

The Fairy Godmother wields her wand. Buttons is calm

Fairy Godmother That's better. Just take a grip on yourself and go and find the Baron to help you.
Buttons (*as he exits calmly*) Find the Baron and just keep cool, man.

Buttons exits

Fairy Godmother Poor lad. Look after him when he needs you, will you?

The Fairy Godmother exits

SCENE 9

The kitchen

The cupboard and Mrs Da Palma are on stage

Mrs Da Palma Cinderella! Darling Cinderella! (*Horrid grin*)

Cinderella enters

Cinderella Yes?
Mrs Da Palma Oh, the Prince is coming to try on the slipper, so I've bought you a lovely new dress to look your best in when you meet him.
Cinderella I don't believe you.
Mrs Da Palma What? Oh, how cruel! I show you the kind warm loving me that lurks beneath this hard shell, and all you do is spurn me. (*Tears*)
Cinderella Well——
Mrs Da Palma It's all right. I know you always think the worst of people.
Cinderella No!
Mrs Da Palma The dress is over there in the cupboard, but I expect you think I'm so horrid that I'm going to trick you.
Cinderella I'll go and have a look. Thank you. I didn't realize you cared about me. (*She goes to the cupboard*)
Mrs Da Palma Oh I do. I love you to death.

She pushes Cinderella into the cupboard

Cinderella (*inside*) Let me out! Let me out! You can't do this to me just when——

The lever is pulled. Silence

Mrs Da Palma Clever old me! Now I can hide it. No-one will find it. I shall become Queen Mother.

She laughs and pushes it off

Buttons creeps on with the Baron

Buttons
Baron } (*together*) Cinderella? Cinderella.

The audience shout

Buttons (*to the audience*) Oh! Oh! (*Not calm*) She's in the cupboard? The silencing lever's been pulled? Then where's she gone? This way? Oh, that way. You go off and search, then, Baron, while I wait for the Prince.

The Baron goes

But if the silencing lever has been pulled, Cinderella won't be able to shout for help, and he won't be able to hear her and so he won't be able to find her and——
Prince (*off*) Hallo!
Buttons Oh, oh! Here's the Prince coming with the slipper and the lovely sisters tottering into the limelight.

They hobble in, Cloaca on crutches and Lymphida with a walking stick

Mrs Da Palma enters

Mrs Da Palma What's wrong with you? (*She kicks away the crutch*) And you too. (*She kicks away the walking stick*)

The sisters cling to each other

Lymphida Mam, is this going to work?
Mrs Da Palma It'd better.

Knock knock

Buttons Hark, a Prince. Calm now, Buttons.
Mrs Da Palma And not a word about anyone else in the house, or else.
Buttons Trust me as you would yourself.

He lets in the Prince, Sam and Jack

Hallo, Royal Party, and especially some of it.
Sam Ooh.
Buttons Welcome to the house of Baron Jones and his unfortunate appendages. (*Whispering*) We're searching for her now.
Prince This is the last place to try, so someone here will have to be it.
Mrs Da Palma Yes indeed, sire. I'll try first, in case it's me.
Prince But you're married.

Mrs Da Palma If the shoe fits, wear it, I always say.

It doesn't

Oh well, saves a divorce.
Prince Thank heavens.
Buttons Lady Cloaca?
Prince Oh Lord.
Cloaca It fits perfectly.
Buttons Just wiggle your toes a bit.
Cloaca I can't.
Prince Why not?
Cloaca She just chopped them off.
Jack Disqualified. It has to be a whole foot.
Mrs Da Palma You never said.
Sam It was understood, wasn't it?
Prince Yes, it was.
Cloaca All that for nothing. What sort of hopeless mother are you?
Lymphida She's lovely. Put it on me, Buttons.
Buttons It won't go.
Mrs Da Palma It will.
Lymphida Stuff it in, go on, stuff it in.
Mrs Da Palma Stuff it in hard.
Lymphida Ow, Mam, it hurts.
Prince It's no good, it has to fit easily.
Lymphida You stupid woman. It's all gone wrong.
Cloaca You're hopeless.
Lymphida Useless.
Cloaca Incompetent.
Mrs Da Palma Silence!

The Baron runs on

Baron We can't find the cupboard, Buttons.
Mrs Da Palma The what?
Baron Nothing.
Mrs Da Palma Don't anyone say a word.
Sisters No.
Jack I will. You have another daughter, Baron.
Prince Oh the grubby one.
Buttons This is it, the Right Moment.
Sam The Right Moment. We have a song for you, Your Highness.

They sing it and the Da Palmas march about saying "Silence" very noisily and singing other songs. Thus the Prince cannot hear. After a few goes, he does and says . . .

Prince Oh, Cinderella.
Buttons Well done everyone.
Prince May I see her, please?
Mrs Da Palma Very well, she's in a cupboard in the dining-room.

Baron (*running off*) Oh, we didn't look in there because it smells so awful.

He runs off

Prince What does it smell of?
Lymphida Me mostly. I'm sick in there a lot.
Mrs Da Palma Little sweetheart.

Cinderella comes in. She is followed by the Baron and the kids with the cupboard. She walks forward to face the Prince

Prince Hallo. Goodness, she is awfully grubby.
Cinderella Do you only judge people by what they look like, Your Highness?
Prince Your voice! It's you! What are you doing here?
Cinderella Just let me try the slipper.
Baron It fits!
Prince It fits!
Baron I knew you were the best daughter in the world.
Cloaca You slimey little greaser.
Lymphida How did it happen, Mam?
Mrs Da Palma I've no idea.
Prince Sam and Jack, I've found her!
Cinderella And do you love me?
Prince With all my heart.
Cinderella And I love you with all my heart as well, all my grubby heart.
Prince Your heart is beautiful, and you are beautiful and I will love you for ever.
Mrs Da Palma Makes you sick.

The Fairy Godmother enters

Fairy Godmother And you can't get married in one shoe so here's the other.
Buttons And I think it's time Mrs Da Palma learnt how to be nice, don't you?
Audience Yes.

Buttons and the kids get her to the cupboard

Mrs Da Palma I won't be nice, I won't, I won't, I won't.
Lymphida What'll we do without you, Mam?
Buttons You'll just have to stand on what's left of your own feet.
Cloaca And be grown up?
Mrs Da Palma I shall never be nice, I shall never be nice, I shall——

The lever is pulled

Buttons Wonderful. Peace, perfect peace.
Cinderella Oh, there are your parents on their way to open a bridge, Hugo. Come into the kitchen, Your Majesties, he's found me.
Prince I've found her.

The King and Queen enter

King I've never been in a kitchen before.
Queen It's where they cook, dear.
King And is this really you?
Prince Yes, it's really her.
King Spendid. Now everything's settled, I've no more use for this. (*He puts his crown on Hugo*)
Queen And I've no use for this. (*She gives her crown to Cinderella*)
King And we can go and pack.
Cinderella The new Prime Minister will help you. Buttons?
Jack Buttons?
Prince Yes, Buttons!
Buttons Oh, jolly good. And the new Prime Minister's wife.
Sam Is this the right moment?
Buttons Yes. We're the power behind the throne now, so all get into line.

Mrs Da Palma bursts out of the cupboard

Mrs Da Palma I am never going to be nice!
Lymphida Oh shut up, Mother and do as you're told.
Cloaca We've learnt a lot from Cinderella.
Mrs Da Palma From her?
Buttons Get into line, and we'll tell you.

Song 19: You Can't Keep a Good Girl Down

(*Singing*)
If you travel down life's highway
And find it awfully grim,
The message of this story
Should light up things when they're dim.
It tells you this and that
Which simply never can be done,
Especially the no-no that
Is no-no number one.

You can't pick your nose with a cricket bat,
You can't boil eggs in glue.
You can't brush your teeth with an angry cat,
You know what'll happen if you do.
You can't mend wellies with cheese on toast,
So shout all over town,
You can't stop a train with a rolling pin,
And you can't keep a good girl down.

Chorus

All
You can't keep a good girl, keep a good girl,
You can't keep a good girl down.
You can't keep a good, can't keep a good, no,
You can't keep a good girl down.
No matter if she's humble
Or blazing with renown,

You can't keep a good girl, keep a good girl,
You can't keep a good girl down.

Verse divided between characters as desired;

You can't keep a parrot in the frigidaire,
You can't make a python jump.
You can't have a snooze on a prickly pear,
Play hockey on a camel's hump.
You can't play chess with a kangaroo,
So shout all over town,
You can't stop a train with a rolling pin,
And you can't keep a good girl down.

Chorus reprise for All

Verse, divided between characters as desired:

You can't go sailing in a baby's pram,
You can't make a tortoise fly.
You can't put a pickle in the strawberry jam,
Pop pepper in a pumpkin pie.
You can't plait fog,
Or eat a dog,
You'll make your grandma frown.
You can't stop a train with a rolling pin,
And you can't keep a good girl down.

All reprise the chorus, the last two lines repeated

CURTAIN

FURNITURE AND PROPERTY LIST

ACT I

SCENE 1

On stage: Bed with bedding
Fireplace

SCENE 2

On stage: 2 thrones on rostrum
Horses **(Sam** and **Jack)**

Off stage: Horse **(Prince)**

SCENE 3

On stage: Horses **(Sam, Jack** and **Prince)**

Off stage: Coffin on cart **(Baron, Buttons, Cinderella)**

Personal: **Prince:** bag of money

SCENE 4

On stage: Nil

Off stage: File, sweets **(Fairy Godmother)**

Personal: **Fairy Godmother:** wand, spectacles on string round neck (*both required throughout*)

SCENE 5

On stage: 2 thrones on rostrum

Off stage: Cupboard with silence lever **(Cloaca** and **Lymphida)**
Bag of money **(Lymphida)**
Horse **(Prince)**

SCENE 6

On stage: Cut-out of house
2 pots of paint
2 brushes

Off stage: Bills **(Baron)**
Cupboard **(Lymphida** and **Cloaca)**
Bag of money **(Lymphida)**
Bedclothes **(Cloaca** and **Lymphida)**

SCENE 7

No props required

SCENE 8

On stage: 2 thrones on rostrum

SCENE 9

On stage: Fireplace
              Stool
              Pots, pans, dishcloth
              Bed with bedding
              Pile of washing
              Bucket, scrubbing brush for **Cinderella**
              Mop

Off stage: Invitations **(Baron)**

SCENE 10

Off stage: Nil

Off stage: 2 invitations **(Sam)**

SCENE 11

On stage: As SCENE 9

Set: Hair brush, combs, etc.
              Invitations

Off stage: Pumpkin **(Cinderella substitute)**
              Coach and 4 horses **(Four Riders)**

Personal: **Riders:** half-masks
              Fairy Godmother: invitation

ACT II

SCENE 1

On stage: Nil

Off stage: Clothes and wigs for boy and girl **(Sam and Jack)**

SCENE 2

On stage: Table with food
              Clock

Personal: **Prince:** medals

SCENE 3

No props required

SCENE 4

On stage: As Act I, SCENE 9

SCENE 5

On stage: 2 thrones on rostrum
Off stage: Slipper **(Prince)**

SCENE 6

On stage: Nil
Off stage: Song sheet **(Stage Management)**

SCENE 7

On stage: Bed
Cupboard

Off stage: Toolbag containing pliers, axe **(Mrs Da Palma)**

Personal: **Lymphida:** trick feet
Cloaca: trick toes

SCENE 8

No props required

SCENE 9

On stage: As Act I, SCENE 9
Set: Cupboard
Off stage: Slipper on cushion **(Prince)**
Cupboard **(Kids)**
Slipper **(Fairy Godmother)**

Personal: **Cloaca:** crutches
Lymphida: walking stick

LIGHTING PLOT

Property fittings required: fire effect, chandelier

Various simple interior and exterior settings

ACT I

To open: Lighting on bedroom, fire effect on

Cue 1	**Buttons:** ". . . more lively there I'll bet!"	(Page 1)
	Crossfade to throne room—bright, general lighting	
Cue 2	At end of Song 1	(Page 4)
	Crossfade to wood—general exterior lighting	
Cue 3	**Buttons:** "Some people."	(Page 7)
	Crossfade to frontcloth lighting	
Cue 4	**Buttons** exit	(Page 10)
	Crossfade to throne room	
Cue 5	**Queen** leaves	(Page 14)
	Crossfade to outside Baron's house	
Cue 6	**Cinderella** (*singing*): "My home away."	(Page 20)
	Crossfade to frontcloth lighting	
Cue 7	**Fairy Godmother** waves frontcloth away	(Page 20)
	Crossfade to lighting on throne room	
Cue 8	**Jack:** "You do have strange ideas at times."	(Page 22)
	Crossfade to kitchen, fire effect on	
Cue 9	**Buttons:** "But not me."	(Page 26)
	Crossfade to frontcloth lighting	
Cue 10	**Buttons:** "Considering."	(Page 27)
	Crossfade to kitchen, fire effect on	
Cue 11	**Fairy Godmother:** "Virtue is going to be rewarded!"	(Page 30)
	Lights for transformation	

ACT II

To open: Frontcloth lighting

Cue 12	**Sam:** "He wasn't invited, was he?"	(Page 32)
	Crossfade to bright general lighting on ballroom, chandelier on	
Cue 13	**Prince** (*singing alone*): "Till the day that I die."	(Page 40)
	Crossfade to frontcloth lighting	

Cue 14	**Jack:** "... what we're going to do next." *Crossfade to kitchen, fire effect on*	(Page 41)
Cue 15	**Buttons** (*singing*): "Till the day that I die." *Crossfade to throne room*	(Page 45)
Cue 16	**Jack:** "... something awful. I know it." *Crossfade to frontcloth lighting*	(Page 47)
Cue 17	**Jack:** "... strikes me as very boring." *Crossfade to bedroom*	(Page 49)
Cue 18	**Mrs Da Palma** (*singing*): "For you're a rat, rat, rat." *Crossfade to frontcloth lighting*	(Page 52)
Cue 19	**Fairy Godmother** exits *Crossfade to kitchen lighting, fire effect on*	(Page 53)

EFFECTS PLOT

ACT I

Cue 1   As SCENE 2 opens   (Page 1)
            Gigantic and jolly trumpets

Cue 2   **King** (*off*): "Here, my love."   (Page 2)
            More trumpets

Cue 3   **King:** "Thank you, that'll do."   (Page 2)
            Cut trumpets

Cue 4   As SCENE 4 opens   (Page 8)
            Flash as **Fairy Godmother** *enters*

Cue 5   **Mrs Da Palma:** "Oh, I'm so sorry." (*She grovels*)   (Page 12)
            Trumpets

Cue 6   **King:** "Stop it."   (Page 12)
            Cut trumpets

Cue 7   **Prince:** "No!"   (Page 21)
            Magic sound; echo effect on **Fairy Godmother**'s *voice*

Cue 8   All shout "Fairy Godmother, Fairy Godmother"   (Page 29)
            Flash as **Fairy Godmother** *enters*

Cue 9   **Fairy Godmother:** "Virtue is going to be rewarded!"   (Page 30)
            Music, thunder, flashes for transformation

ACT II

Cue 10   **Sam:** "... come near them."   (Page 34)
            Trumpets

Cue 11   **Buttons:** "... Most Beautiful of All."   (Page 35)
            More trumpets

Cue 12   **Cloaca:** "... poison in her caviare."   (Page 38)
            Clock begins to strike 12

Cue 13   **Fairy Godmother:** "... to see how you're getting on."   (Page 43)
            Flash as she exits

Cue 14   **Mrs Da Palma:** "It'd better."   (Page 54)
            Knock knock

MADE AND PRINTED IN GREAT BRITAIN BY
LATIMER TREND & COMPANY LTD PLYMOUTH

MADE IN ENGLAND